how many animals were on the ARK?

Understanding the Animal Kinds

general editor: Craig Froman

First printing: July 2016
Second printing: November 2016

Master Books® is a division of the
New Leaf Publishing Group, Inc.

ISBN: 978-0-89051-935-6
Library of Congress Number: 2016908609

Cover & Interior Design by Diana Bogardus

Unless otherwise noted, Scripture quotations are from the New King James Version of the Bible.

Please consider requesting that a copy of this volume be purchased by your local library system.

Printed in China

Please visit our website for other great titles:
www.masterbooks.com

For information regarding author interviews, please contact the publicity department at (870) 438-5288

Except for chapter 2, these chapters are adapted from articles on the Answers in Genesis website: www. answersingenesis.org

Master
Books®
A Division of New Leaf Publishing Group
www.masterbooks.com

Introduction
by Ken Ham

We have all seen the images of the bathtub Noah's Ark with giraffes sticking their necks out of the windows, and a few other pairs of animals hanging out with Noah, all with big grins on their faces. Something about it seems sweet, but more from a fairytale than a real account of faith and survival. How could an ancient boat carry millions of animal species in order to repopulate the entire planet across such wild waves of water? Is that even scientifically possible?

Most children and teens in today's church learn about the "real" things of science—things that can be physically analyzed and touched (i.e., fossils, rocks, etc.)—from an evolutionary framework. It's no wonder, then, that these young people believe that the Bible's history is wrong, thus leading many of them to conclude that the Bible is irrelevant and untrustworthy. That's one reason America's Research Group conducted research on what people in America believe about the Bible. On the subject of Noah's Ark, 86 percent of those in their 60s believed that Noah's Ark was actually built, but only 52 percent of those in their 20s believed this.

Noah's Ark

Yes, the real Ark had to carry considerably more animals than a few giraffes and elephants, and with cages and pens enough to keep them safe, along with food for Noah, his family, and all these animals for this long journey, tools, other provisions, seeds, and more. Well, don't scientists tell us there are anywhere between 2 or 3 million species or maybe more on earth? How could 8 people possibly care for that many animals and birds, and how could any boat ever carry them for a year or more?

You're about to take a journey back to the powerful Flood that reshaped the earth, and discover some of the mysteries of God's remarkable creation. And you will also see how some terms that scientists use actually make things seem much more difficult and confusing than they need to be. Just how many animals did Noah and his family actually carry on the Ark? We don't know the exact number, because some have become extinct, but you'll find it's not really as many as some might think.

Fewer and fewer people seem to believe in the historical truth of the Bible, and the accounts of history in the book of Genesis are being questioned more each day, even by people in the church. This book was written to help answer some of the questions and concerns of those who can't quite seem to grasp the whole truth of Noah's Ark, and to strengthen the faith of those who already do.

By faith Noah, being divinely warned of things not yet seen, moved with godly fear, prepared an ark for the saving of his household, by which he condemned the world and became heir of the righteousness which is according to faith. (Hebrews 11:7)

1 Did all animals really come from a single animal long ago?

[Cheetah]

[Lion]

[House Cat]

[Jaguar]

GENETIC POTENTIAL

CATS ARE...CATS! According to Genesis 1, God made each type of creature "according to its kind." Within their DNA, God placed the potential for tremendous variety, including new species. But every species belongs to its original kind—cats are still cats, and dogs are dogs.

[Original Created Cat Kind]

WHAT EXACTLY IS A "KIND"? Our world is filled with a tremendous variety of life. And its origin is no mystery. The Bible says God created every kind of living thing on Days Three, Five, and Six of Creation Week. Ten times in Genesis 1 the phrase "according to its [or their] kind" is used in connection with different types of plants and animals. The word *kind* is used again in Genesis 6 when God instructed Noah to take two of every kind of land animal onto the Ark (and seven pairs of some); and in Genesis 8 God commanded these animals to reproduce after the Flood.

Since two of each kind of land animal (and seven pairs of some) were brought aboard the Ark for the purpose of preserving their offspring upon the earth (Genesis 7:3), it seems clear that a "kind" represents the basic boundary of a living thing. That is, the offspring of a living thing is always the same kind as its parents, even though it may have different features.

[**STANDARD POODLE** + **LABRADOR** = **LABRADOODLE**]

GONE TO THE DOGS! Dogs exhibit tremendous variety. Yet diverse breeds of dogs can produce offspring with each other—indicating that all dogs are of the same kind. Dogs will not interbreed with cats, however, since they are a different kind. Modern breeding research therefore confirms the biblical concept of animal and plant kinds.

ZEBRA + DONKEY = ZONKEY

Creation researchers have found that "kind" is often at the level of "family" in the modern way we classify animals. For example, zebras, horses, and donkeys all belong to the family Equidae and can mate with each other to form hybrid animals such as mules (from a donkey and horse) and zonkeys (from a zebra and donkey).

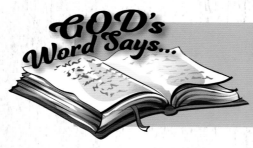

GOD's Word Says...

And God made the beast of the earth according to its kind, cattle according to its kind, and everything that creeps on the earth according to its kind. And God saw that it was good. (Genesis 1:25)

God placed the potential for tremendous variety within the original created kinds. This original created genetic diversity, in addition to mutations and other mechanisms after the Fall (such as natural selection), led to the great diversity of living things we see today.

BARA-WHAT? A modern field of study, called baraminology (from the two Hebrew words *bara,* meaning "created," and *min,* meaning "kind"), attempts to classify fossil and living organisms into their original created kinds (or baramins). As creation scientists, we are not ashamed to stand on the foundation of God's Word for our research and understanding of living things. More on this later in the book!

[BARA $+$ MIN $=$ BARAMINOLOGY]

penguin kind

bushbaby kind

rabbit kind

iguana kind

SO REMEMBER! Genesis 1 repeats ten times that God created creatures separately according to various "kinds." Today's species show the potential variation that God designed within the original kinds, but this variety remains limited—cats are still cats, and dogs are dogs.

2 Who is Carl Linnaeus, and what did he have to do with animal kinds?

The familiar system of scientific naming was developed by a creationist and biologist, Carl Linnaeus (lih-NEE-us), who developed the "two-name naming system" (or if you prefer, "binomial nomenclature!"). Each kind was given a broader name, the genus, followed by a more specific species name (e.g., *Homo sapiens* for human beings). The broader genus name is given first and capitalized, followed by the narrower species name in lower case, both in italics. This works with mountain lions as well: *Puma concolor!*

GOD's Word Says...

All flesh is not the same flesh, but there is one kind of flesh of men, another flesh of animals, another of fish, and another of birds. (1 Corinthians 15:39)

Scientists recognize that biological classification involves several types of grouping techniques. One is recognizing and naming the true scientific species. Many scientists still use the system devised by Linnaeus in the 1700s, which is based on the ability to interbreed, as the primary basis for assigning genus-species scientific names. The part of biological classification that emphasizes giving proper scientific names to organisms is called "taxonomy."

ORDER TO GO! Carl Linnaeus truly saw order in nature. He deeply valued God's Word and believed the Bible when it stated that God was the Creator of all things.

Linnaeus also gave us a series of taxonomic ranks for grouping created kinds into a series of categories that you may be familiar with: family, order, class, phylum (or division in plants), and kingdom. Examples illustrating Linnaeus' classification are shown on the next few pages. Those who believe in evolution tried to pirate Linnaeus' system, substituting made-up common ancestors for the variation in God's creatures.

Linnaeus laid a firm foundation on which other scientists could build. Scientists could apply his rules for naming plants to animals, too. For instance, all cats belong to the family Felidae. Scientists give a separate name for each species of cat. The jaguar is *Panthera onca*; mountain lion is *Puma concolor*; and leopard is *Panthera pardus*.

YOU CALL A MOUNTAIN LION A WHAT?

The biological classification goes from the general to the specific. Each plant and animal has a unique name that is shared by no other. The classification for mountain lion, *Puma concolor*, is:

MOUNTAIN LION	
Kingdom	Animalia
Phylum	Chordata (animal with a nerve cord)
Class	Mammalia (mother provides milk for the young)
Order	Carnivora (eats flesh)
Family	Felidae (cat)
Genus	*Puma* (an Inca name)
Species	*P. concolor* (one color)

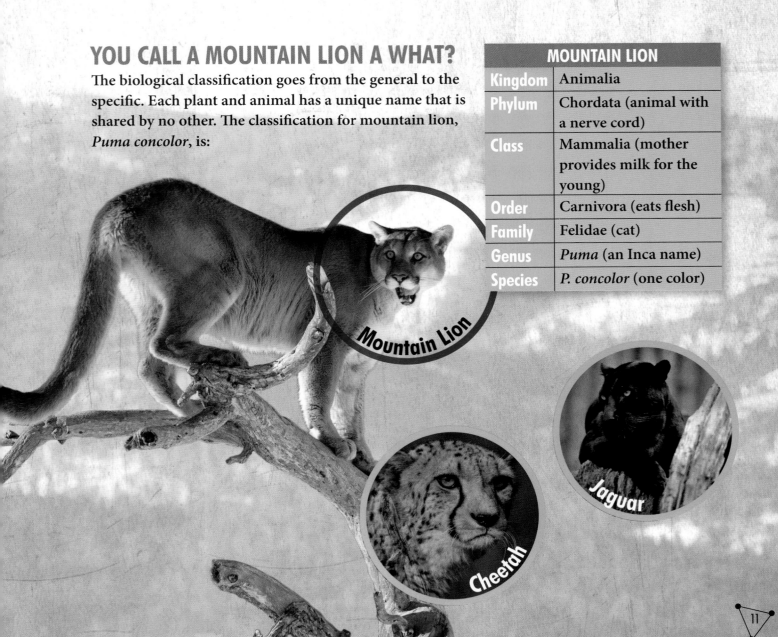

Mountain Lion

Cheetah

Jaguar

TAXO-WHO? The taxonomic rankings shown in the chart were first suggested by Linnaeus in the 1700s, and are still often used by scientists today. Taxonomy is just a fancy word for sorting or classifying living things. And classification is simply the practice of sorting similar subjects together. A good classification system of animals and plants should start with the account of Creation in Genesis.

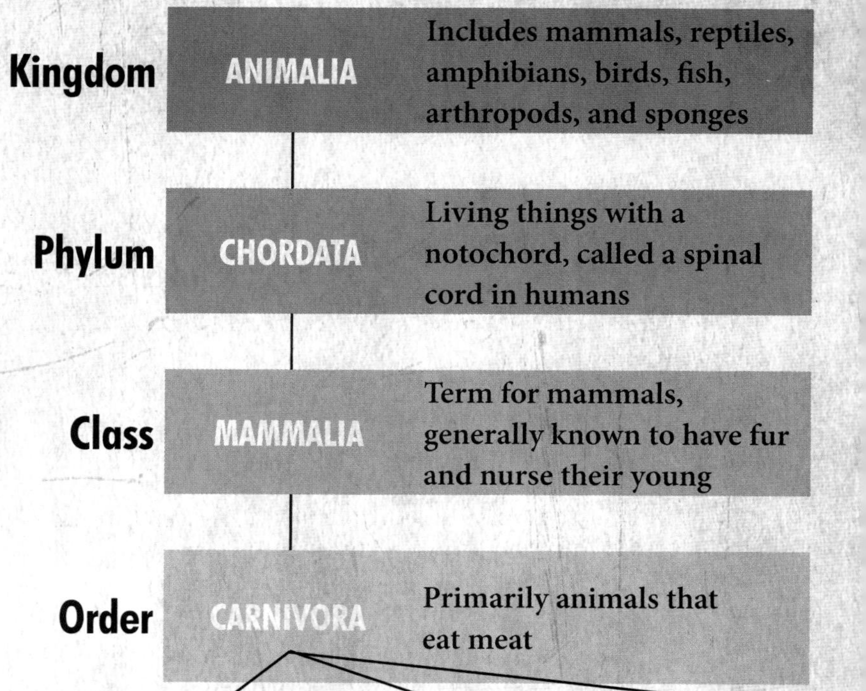

Kingdom — ANIMALIA — Includes mammals, reptiles, amphibians, birds, fish, arthropods, and sponges

Phylum — CHORDATA — Living things with a notochord, called a spinal cord in humans

Class — MAMMALIA — Term for mammals, generally known to have fur and nurse their young

Order — CARNIVORA — Primarily animals that eat meat

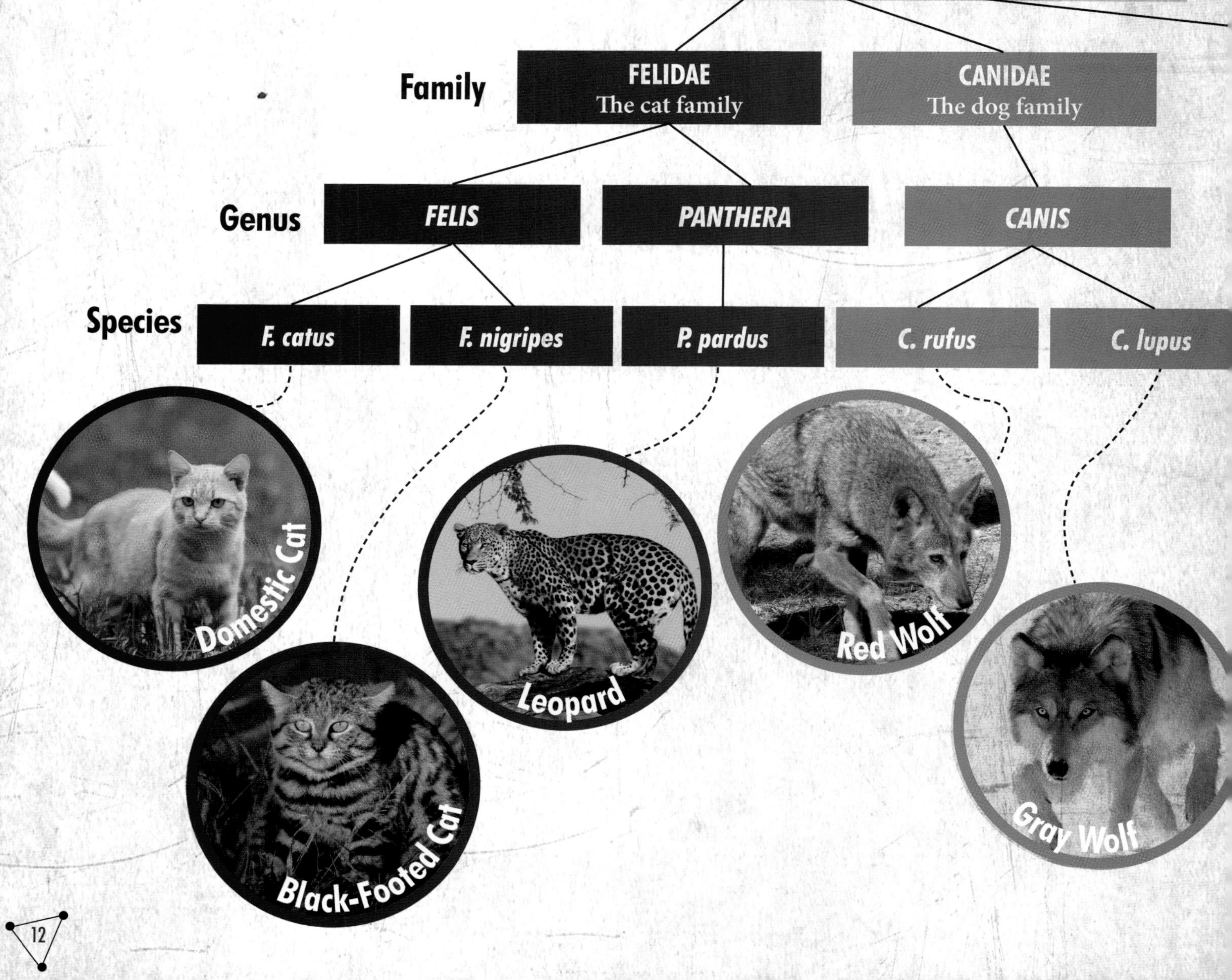

Family — FELIDAE — The cat family — CANIDAE — The dog family

Genus — FELIS — PANTHERA — CANIS

Species — F. catus — F. nigripes — P. pardus — C. rufus — C. lupus

Domestic Cat

Black-Footed Cat

Leopard

Red Wolf

Gray Wolf

SO REMEMBER! Carl Linnaeus believed his classification idea simply showed the order that God had already put in nature when He created the universe. Linnaeus always spoke of the species as "the created kinds," though creation scientists today know that the level of "family" is a better approximation of kind. Linnaeus developed a way to name plants and animals so that each living thing would have a unique — one-of-a-kind — name, and it's still used today!

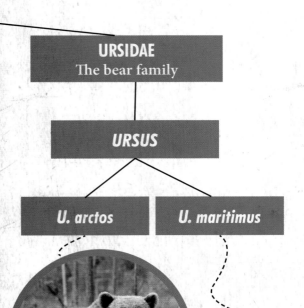

URSIDAE
The bear family

URSUS

U. arctos **U. maritimus**

Brown Bear

Polar Bear

CLASSIFICATION SYSTEMS

A garden, orchard, or huge field of small bushes might be used to represent a good classification system for a creationist. This would show many separately created kinds, each showing variation within its kind. Evolutionary beliefs about classification are usually represented as a "tree of life." This evolutionary tree (quite different from the one in Genesis!) is meant to suggest continuity among all living things. With gradual changes progressing along branching lines of descent, it moves from one common ancestor to the multitude of separate species ("branch tips") they show today.

Let's look at mammals, for example, a group defined as animals that nourish their young on milk (from mammary glands). Whether they run (horses), swim (whales), fly (bats), or burrow (moles), or whether they are large (elephants) or small (mice), each mammal is 100 percent mammal. So within the mammalian class or "box" are smaller "boxes," mammalian subgroups separated from each other by features considered to have less significance than milk production. Some types of these subgroups include those with membranous wings (bats, order *Chiroptera*), swimming mammals with blowholes (whales and dolphins, order *Cetacea*), and hoofed animals (ungulates) with an odd number of toes (e.g., horses, order *Perissodactyla*).

3 What are the "kinds" in the Book of Genesis?

"Zonkeys, Ligers, and Wholphins, Oh My!" Although not exactly the same line that the travelers in the classic *Wizard of Oz* repeat, these names represent real life animals just the same. In May of 2008, The Creation Museum petting zoo acquired two such animals—a zonkey and a zorse! But what exactly are these animals, and how did they come to be? Are they new species? Can the Bible explain such a thing?

A good rule of thumb is that if two things can breed together, then they are of the same created kind. It is a bit more complicated than this, but for the time being, this is a quick measure of a "kind." Evidence to support this concept is clearly seen (or rather not seen) in our world today, as there are no reports of dats (dog + cat) or hows (horse + cow)!

[DOG + CAT = DATS?]

Cat Kind

Elephant Kind

Sheep Kind

Kangaroo Kind

QUICK MEASURE OF A "KIND"! Often, people are confused into thinking that a "species" is a "kind." But this isn't necessarily so. A "species" is a man-made term used in the *modern* classification system. And frankly, the word *species* is difficult to define, whether one is a creationist or not! The Bible uses the term "kind." The Bible's first use of this word (Hebrew: *min*) is found in Genesis 1 when God creates plants and animals "according to their kinds." It is used again in Genesis 6 and 8 when God instructs Noah to take two of every kind of land-dwelling, air-breathing animal (and seven pairs of some) onto the Ark and also in God's command for the animals to fill the earth after the Flood.

Labrador

German Shepherd

Coyote

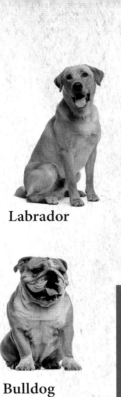
Bulldog

Beagle

Australian Shepherd

Let's take another look at dogs as an example of the created kind. Dogs can easily breed with one another, whether wolves, dingoes, coyotes, or domestic dogs. When dogs breed together, you get dogs; so there is a dog kind. The concept is fairly easy to understand.

Rottweiler

Dachshund

French Bulldog

Wolf

Chihuahua

Shih Tzu

Great Dane

English Cocker

Quack Terrier

[Wait, what?]

Bernese Mountain

Dingo

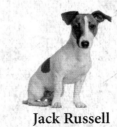
Jack Russell

Doberman Pinscher

But in today's culture, where evolution and millions of years are taught as fact, many people have been led to believe that animals and plants (that are classed as a specific "species") have been like this for tens of thousands of years and perhaps millions of years. So when they see things like lions or zebras, they think they have been like this for an extremely long time.

From a biblical perspective, though, land animals like wolves, zebras, sheep, lions, and so on each have at least two ancestors that lived on Noah's Ark, only about 4,300 years ago. These animals have undergone many changes since that time. But dogs are still part of the dog kind, cats are still part of the cat kind, and so on.

[**Dutch-Booted Bantam**] [**Pheasant**] [**Kraienköppe**] [**Turkey**]

[**Phoenix**]   **This amazing variety of birds all belong to the landfowl kind.**

HEY, WHAT EXACTLY IS BARAMINOLOGY?

Baraminology is a field of study that attempts to classify fossil and living organisms into baramins or kinds.

Because none of the original ancestors survive today, creationists have been trying to figure out what descendants belong to each baramin in their varied forms. Baramin is commonly believed to be at the level of family and possibly order for some plants/animals (according to the common classification system of kingdom, phylum, class, order, family, genus, species). On rare occasions, a kind may be closer to the genus or species levels.

[**Variety in Landfowl Feathers**]

BARA-WHO? Creation scientists use the word *baramin* to refer to created kinds.

BARA	MIN	OLOGY
Hebrew: *BARA*	Hebrew: *Min*	**A SUBJECT**
CREATED	**KIND**	**OF STUDY**

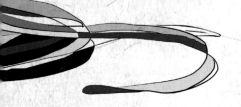

Trying to classify living things into baramins is done based on many criteria, such as ability to form hybrids and physical characteristics. For living organisms, hybridization is the key criteria. If two animals can produce a hybrid, then they are considered to be of the same kind.[1] However, the inability to produce offspring does not necessarily rule out that the animals are of the same kind, since this may be the result of mutations (since the Fall).

Consider some of the following amazing animal hybrids.

HEY, WHAT EXACTLY IS A "HYBRID"? Hybrids are animals that are created from mixing two different parents of the same kind. A female horse that is mated with a male donkey produces a baby that is called a mule.

Horses of all shapes and sizes are of the same kind.

Belgian Heavy Draught

Fjord Pony

Orlov Trotter

Shetland Pony

Bring out with you every living thing of all flesh that is with you: birds and cattle and every creeping thing that creeps on the earth, so that they may abound on the earth, and be fruitful and multiply on the earth. (Genesis 8:17)

The concept of "kind" is important for understanding how Noah fit all the animals on the Ark. If kind is typically at the level of family/order, there would have been plenty of room on the Ark to take two of every kind and seven pairs of some. For example, even though many different dinosaurs have been identified, creation scientists think there are only about 60-80 "kinds" of dinosaurs. Even though breeding studies are impossible with dinosaurs, by studying fossils one can ascertain that there was likely one ceratopsid kind, with variation in that kind.

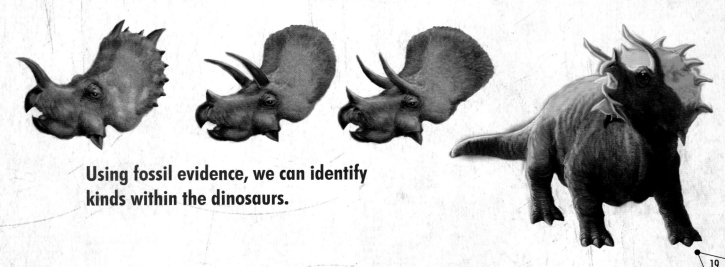

Using fossil evidence, we can identify kinds within the dinosaurs.

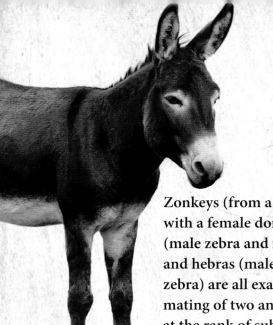

Zonkeys (from a male zebra bred with a female donkey), zorses (male zebra and female horse), and hebras (male horse and female zebra) are all examples of hybrid animals. Hybrid animals are the result of the mating of two animals of the same "kind," but only if the contributing parties differ at the rank of subspecies or higher. Perhaps one of the most popular hybrids of the past has been the mule, the mating of a horse and donkey. So seeing something like a zorse or zonkey shouldn't really surprise anyone, since donkeys, zebras, and horses all belong to the horse kind.

ZONKEYS, ZORSES, AND MULES These hybrids are the result of mating within the family Equidae. As we've said before, zonkeys are the result of mating a male zebra and a female donkey; zorses are the result of mating a male zebra and a female horse; and mules are the result of mating a male donkey and a female horse. But reverse matings (such as hinnies produced from a male horse and female donkey) are rare, although still possible. All are considered "infertile" due to uneven chromosome numbers, but fertility has been observed in some cases. Zonkeys and zorses have a mixture of their parents' traits, including the beautiful striping patterns of the zebra parents.

WHOLPHIN Turning to the ocean, this hybrid is the result of mating within the family Delphinidae. The wholphin is the result of mating a false killer whale (genus *Pseudorca*) and bottlenose dolphin (genus *Tursiops*). Such a mating occurred in captivity at Hawaii's Sea Life Park in 1985.[2] The wholphin is fertile. This hybrid shows the difficulty of determining the species designation, since a major criteria is the ability to interbreed and produce fertile offspring. Even though the whale and dolphin are considered separate genera, they may, in fact, belong to the same genera. This shows how difficult it is to define the terms genus and species. Of course, from a biblical perspective it is easy to say they are both the same kind!

Wholphin

Liger

Leopard-Jaguar Hybrid

Tigon

Savannah Cat

LIGERS, TIGONS, AND OTHER CATS

These hybrids are the result of mating within the family Felidae. Ligers are the result of mating a male lion and a female tiger. Ligers are the largest cats in the world, weighing in at over 1,000 pounds (450 kg). Tigons are the result of mating a male tiger and a female lion. These matings only occur in captivity, since lions live in Africa, tigers live in Asia, and the two are enemies in the wild. Female hybrids are typically fertile, while male hybrids are not.

Other hybrids in this family include bobcats that mate with domestic cats and bobcats with lynx (Blynx and Lynxcat). There have been mixes of the cougar and the ocelot, as well as many others. This shows that large, midsize, and small cats can ultimately interbreed and therefore suggests that there is only one cat kind.

Eurasian Lynx (*Lynx lynx*)

Bobcat (*Lynx rufus*)

IT'S ALL LATIN TO ME!

It made sense to Carl Linnaeus to begin using Latin terms for his new classification system. The words *species* and *genus* were used for the Hebrew word *min* or kind.

Dog [Latin: *Canis*]
Optimum hominis amicus
[Man's Best Friend]

2 LATIN WORDS	HEBREW WORD
[GENUS **&** SPECIES ⇄	MIN OR KIND]

It was logical to use these common terms, which were a part of the commercial language throughout Europe (much in the way that English, for example, is seen as a universal language in the world today). Linnaeus even wrote his large treatise, *Systema Natvrae,* and other findings, in Latin in the mid to late 1700s. After Linnaeus, both of these words (genus and species) were commonly used in modern biological classification systems with slightly different definitions.

[**THEN** One dog species]

Original definition of species: all dogs were one species.

Gray Wolf   African Wild Dog   Black-backed Jackal   Arctic Fox   Raccoon Dog   Dog

HOW DID THAT HAPPEN?

In the mid to late 1700s, species began taking on a new, more specific definition in scientific circles as a biological term. But, by and large, the definition had changed so that instead of there being a dog species or a dog kind, there were many dog species.

[**NOW** Several dog species]

ONE CREATED KIND Every modern member of the elephant "kind" has the same basic features – a long trunk, tusks, and floppy ears. And though there are differences, from size (African bush elephants are the largest land animals), to preferred food (the African bush elephants eat mostly grasses, while the African forest elephants eat mostly leaves and bark), and the size of their ears (Asian elephants have the smallest ears of any elephant), they are all representatives of the elephant kind.

African Forest Elephant

African Bush Elephant

Asian Elephant

The word *species* was viewed for a long time as the biblical "kind." But as the scientific term changed and gained popularity, this led to a problem. When theologians and other members of the church talked about species (they were still meaning it in terms of the old definition), people readily saw that there were variations among the species (by the new definition). They thought, "But species do change!" Of course, no one ever demonstrated something like a dog changing into something like a cat. Dogs were still dogs, cats were still cats, and so on.

Even today, one objection to the Bible is that it claims that species are fixed, meaning they never change. A good response would be: "To which

definition of species are you referring?" By the old definition (as a kind), creationists would agree, but would probably better state it in modern English as fixity of the created kinds so as not to confuse the issue. The idea of one kind changing into another has never been observed. All of these animals' ancestors that we have discussed—horses, donkeys, zebras, tigers, lions, whales, and dolphins—were created with genetic diversity within their various kinds. Through time, reshuffling of created genetic diversity, mutation, natural selection and other processes have altered the original information to give us even more variation within a kind.

SO REMEMBER! Great variety can be observed in the offspring of animals of the same kind, just as the same cake recipe can be used to make many different cakes, including sheet cakes, cupcakes, or round cakes. Hybrids have a portion of the same genetic information as their parents but combined in a unique way to give a very unique-looking animal. What an amazing diversity of life God has created for us to enjoy!

4   What can a dog's life tell us about kinds?

The American hairless terrier is one of the newer official dog breeds, recognized by the United Kennel Club in 2004. Just in time, too. Allergies have reached epidemic proportions, forcing many sufferers to miss out on one of life's basic pleasures. Now an adorable dog is available for them, too—the perfect lap size and no shedding. These dogs' natural intelligence and calm temperament make them excellent companions. They are also curious, active, courageous, and playful. Humans had a need, and presto, we could breed a dog to meet those needs. Just coincidence?

Centuries ago, English breeders saw another need—a massive dog that could guard, do search and rescue, and assist police work. So the English mastiff was born. It is, in fact, the heaviest breed on record, the largest one tipping the scale at 343 pounds (156 kg). These gentle giants have an amiable nature. They love families and desire to please.

How could any two animals be more different? And these are just two of the 500 domestic dog breeds around the world!

American Hairless Terrier

English Mastiff

Miniature Horse

YOU GOTTA BE KIDDING ME!

Does it amaze you that the vast majority of the 500 dog breeds are fewer than 500 years old? Indeed, most are fewer than 150 years old. Biologists are puzzled by how so many varieties have been produced in such a short time. As a matter of fact, no other mammal has the same range of variation.[1]

How could these diverse traits appear so quickly, rather than by slow, chance processes over thousands of generations? The only reasonable explanation for such complex, elegant, genetic systems is that they were designed that way.

GOD's Word Says...

For since the creation of the world His invisible attributes are clearly seen, being understood by the things that are made, even His eternal power and Godhead, so that they are without excuse. (Romans 1:20)

ORIGIN OF DOGS FROM WOLVES

Charles Darwin, just like the rest of us, must have seen the Creator in the creatures all around him even though he denied Him. Several dog breeds were always at his side, but his favorite was Polly, a terrier. Despite loving his pets dearly and constantly marveling at their personalities and abilities, Darwin was unwilling to credit their origin with the Creator. Why? In a series of correspondences with his Christian friend Asa Gray, Darwin discussed why he didn't believe variation

within species was divinely designed.[2] Like many Christian biologists in his day, Gray believed life had existed for eons of time and rejected Genesis's teaching that God's "very good" creation was corrupted by Adam's sin. So Darwin showed Gray the logical consequence of his view. If death and suffering were always a part of nature, then his "god" must be unfeeling and distant, and he didn't trifle with details like species variation. Gray had difficulty disputing Darwin's claim.

Yet Darwin and the scientific community at that time had no understanding of the complex genetics required to produce variation. Consequently, Darwin thought it should be easy to explain species variation by random natural processes without divine design, and he expected experiments with artificial breeding to prove his point. But they never did.

Today, research in genetics is exploding, and scientists are beginning to see just how much is involved in producing and inheriting traits. While our understanding of the immense chemical and genetic systems necessary to coordinate this diversity has increased by leaps and bounds, researchers recognize that they are seeing only the tip of the iceberg.

Dogs are the focus of ongoing research to solve the mystery of vast variations within a kind over a short amount of time. Historically, it was assumed that domestic dogs (*Canis lupus familiaris*) were only recently derived from the gray wolf (*Canis lupus*). As humans began to settle down and farm, wolves supposedly co-evolved with people over thousands of years. But how do you make a domestic dog out of killer wolf? It requires more than changing hair color!

DOMESTICATING ANIMALS!

The study of domesticating or taming animals has been broken down into two major categories: biological changes and behavioral changes. Researchers believe genetically-based behavioral differences were present when humans took animals out of the wild population. These animals were then bred to develop tamer varieties. During this process, genetic changes occurred. Cultural changes also ensued, as humans incorporated the early dogs into their society, either as assistant hunters or scrap eaters. People from different cultures prized different traits, depending on their religious, economic, and work needs. Evolutionary teaching states that it takes thousands of years for minor changes to occur.

As dogs became more domesticated, many came to depend on scraps for survival, no longer using their hunting instincts. Some were actually bred to be gentle family pets.

But a 2014 study is forcing researchers to rethink this scenario.[3] Until recently, most researchers believed humans living in the Middle East, Europe, and China adopted local wolves into their separate cultures. So they expected the genes of these local dogs to be more similar to those of local wolves than to dogs on other continents.

The study found that old dog breeds, no matter what continent they live on, are more similar to each other than to wolves living nearby. This is amazing because it indicates that all dogs came from the same stock after they diverged from modern wolves. In other words, an early population of dogs was living in a single region at the same time that gray wolves were spreading over the earth. Humans living in this region possibly took the dogs with them as they spread over the earth; or the dogs moved out on their own, later to be domesticated.

The limited amount of fossil and archaeological evidence makes it difficult to confirm these implications from the recent gene studies. Gray wolves don't appear in the fossil record until about 100 years after Noah's Flood. Indeed, the gray wolf is only one out of 35 living species in the Canidae family.[4] "Dogs" don't appear in the fossil record until the end of the Ice Age, sometime after gray wolves, foxes, and their other relatives.

Many recognize that it would be very difficult to tell when the first dogs were domesticated because their anatomy would be wolf-like. For example, at least one late Ice Age site in Europe contained a wolf buried in a cemetery similar to a cemetery for humans. Was this an early "dog"? Researchers hypothesize that there were probably not a lot of physical changes from the wolf to the early dogs. This understanding would explain why "dog" artifacts do not appear until near the end of the Ice Age, about 4,000 years ago.

THE CREATION OF THE CANIDAE KIND

The Bible leaves no doubt about the ultimate origin of dogs, wolves, and their kin. On Day Six, God created the land animals, each according to their kinds; and He made Adam and Eve, too. Those kinds would include the original parents of the Canidae family, which produced both wolves and dogs.

God told the original kinds to "be fruitful and multiply" (Genesis 1:22, 1:28). Being fruitful and multiplying may allude to more than increasing animal numbers; animal diversity would also increase as creatures adapted to varied environments.[5] The diversity certainly increased among the kinds that left the Ark: we find at least 127 post-Flood species (both living and extinct) in the dog/wolf family alone, which arose from the first parents on the Ark.

Silver Fox

We still do not have sufficient evidence to settle whether the human population at Babel had already begun domesticating animals from the Canidae family, but it is intriguing to consider.

When we ponder the modern field of genetics in light of the Creator, we recognize that the field itself is a testimony to the Bible's historical account of origins. Research suggests that the genes reflect a complex biochemical language that is so intricate that we are just scratching the surface of what it means and how it affects species variation. This genetic information has been likened to computer programming but better—more intricate and multidimensional than the best human minds have ever conceived.

That is just what we would expect from the infinite Author of life, God, who is known as the Word, and who desires to communicate with His image-bearers about His invisible attributes (Romans 1:20). Those wonderful attributes are clear for those who have eyes to see.

The very existence of genetic programs that help produce such vast variation within each created kind speaks of the Creator. Such genetic variability is evident throughout nature, such as in the orchid family. It is probably the largest flower family in the world, with thousands of wild species filling the earth since Noah's Flood. Yet through the process of artificially selecting desired traits, humans have bred thousands—perhaps hundreds of thousands—of new varieties not found in the wild.

By God's gracious design of created genetic diversity, artificial selection allows us to reveal variety never before seen. Mixing different varieties, whether orchids or dogs, continually brings new combinations to light.

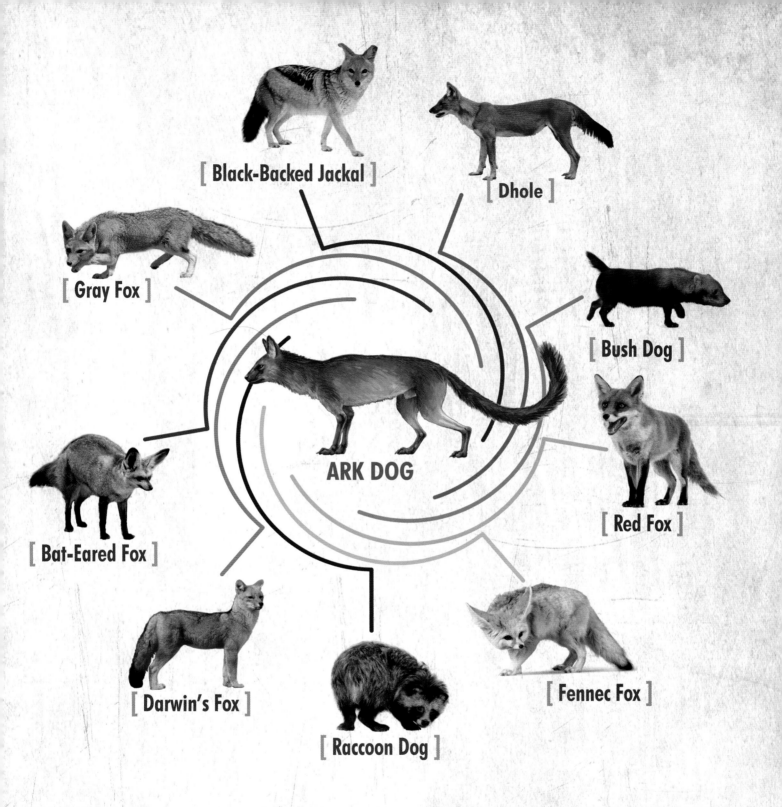

[Black-Backed Jackal]

[Dhole]

[Gray Fox]

[Bush Dog]

ARK DOG

[Bat-Eared Fox]

[Red Fox]

[Darwin's Fox]

[Raccoon Dog]

[Fennec Fox]

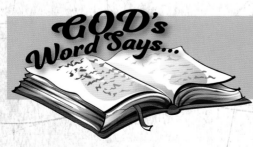

Red Fox

Black-Backed Jackal

Raccoon Dog

Gray Fox

Bat Eared Fox

Arctic Fox

Kit Fox

Biologists have been trying for decades to get to the bottom of this astonishing variability, especially in dogs, which are more varied than any other animal, whether domestic or wild. (Cats don't come close.) An enterprising researcher in Russia decided to see what would happen if he tried to domesticate a second wild animal from the Canidae family—a silver variant of red foxes (*Vulpes vulpes*). For more than 50 years, his laboratory tested how quickly the genetic variety in silver foxes could be revealed during the slow process of domestication. The goal was to recreate the evolutionary processes hypothesized to take tens of thousands of years to change wolves into dogs. The researchers began by selecting 130 of the calmest foxes they could find.

Thousands of years would not be considered a long time to evolutionists; in fact, many consider it "quick." So imagine their surprise when, in just a few years, floppy-eared foxes with wagging tails were born. In just a dozen or so generations, these wild carnivores were friendly to strangers, loved to be petted, desired to be held, and were born with spotted or chestnut-colored fur. These traits are characteristic of domesticated dogs.

Because evolutionary scientists are trained to leave the Creator out of the equation, they assume dogs needed tens of thousands of years of natural selection acting on random mutations to produce changes. Using artificial selection, as breeders do, they assumed they could compress this change into a shorter time, but not this short! The results were "startling," "extraordinary," and "miraculous."[6]

Another line of research is trying to locate the genes involved with these rapid changes. What has come to light is that, once one trait is selected, other traits are affected, too. Changes appear in vast, interrelated suites that appear all at once. It's hard to identify a separate gene for each separate trait. A *National Geographic* article explains, "Identifying the precise genetic footprint involved in tameness . . . is proving extremely tricky science. First the researchers need to find the genes responsible for creating friendly and aggressive behaviors. Such general behavior traits, however, are actually combinations of more specific ones— fear, boldness, passivity, curiosity—

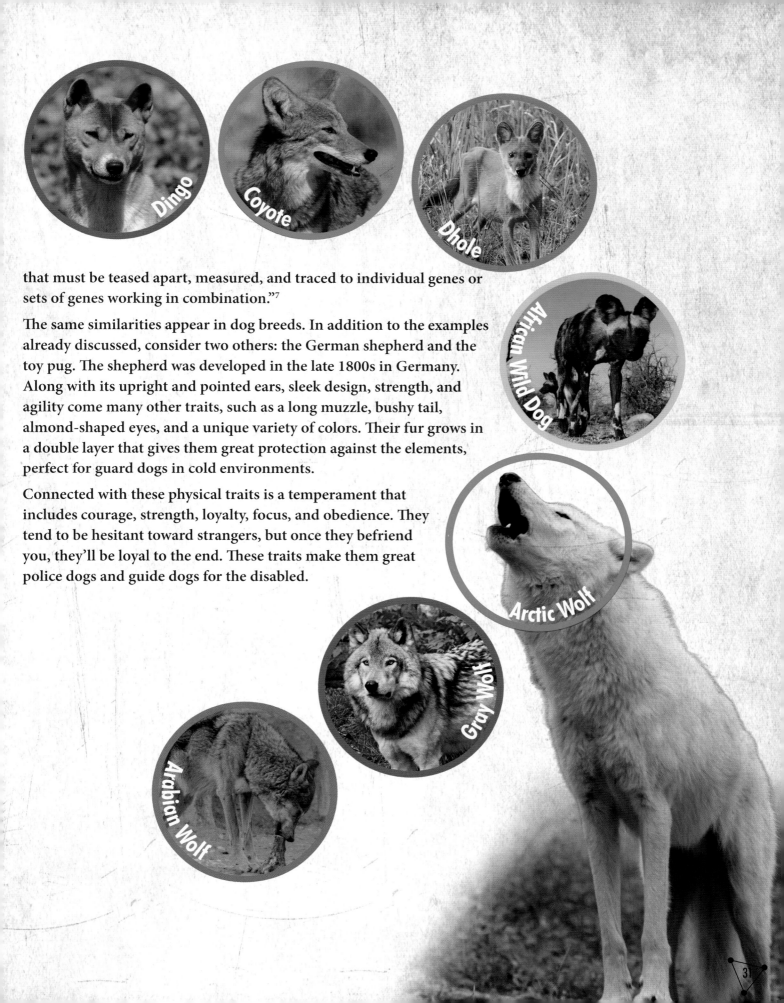

that must be teased apart, measured, and traced to individual genes or sets of genes working in combination."[7]

The same similarities appear in dog breeds. In addition to the examples already discussed, consider two others: the German shepherd and the toy pug. The shepherd was developed in the late 1800s in Germany. Along with its upright and pointed ears, sleek design, strength, and agility come many other traits, such as a long muzzle, bushy tail, almond-shaped eyes, and a unique variety of colors. Their fur grows in a double layer that gives them great protection against the elements, perfect for guard dogs in cold environments.

Connected with these physical traits is a temperament that includes courage, strength, loyalty, focus, and obedience. They tend to be hesitant toward strangers, but once they befriend you, they'll be loyal to the end. These traits make them great police dogs and guide dogs for the disabled.

SWEET TOY PUG! The pug was developed over 2,000 years ago in China, while the "toy" variety was not officially recognized by the American Kennel Association until 1885. With their tiny stature, curly tail (sometimes double curled), bulging eyes, flattened snout, and black face mask, they are a sight to behold! Their fur coat is smooth and usually one color. They were bred for lifelong human companionship and do not usually do well with hunting, fetching, or guarding. They are content sitting on your lap and vying for your affection.

The vast differences between any two dog breeds are more amazing when you consider they are all the same subspecies (*Canis lupus familiaris*). Many other animals have been domesticated rapidly, as well. These domestic animals include fish, sheep, cows, pigs, chickens, and rats. Interestingly, each kind has a similar set of traits (technically known as a "domestication phenotype") that allows humans to work with them. The rapidity and complexity of genetic changes necessary to produce "suites of traits" place seemingly insurmountable obstacles against the idea that these helpful animal varieties come from random mutations.

Our knowledge of the genetic "language" and breeding experiments point clearly to the intentional design of God, who gave His creatures tremendous initial genetic diversity with the genetic flexibility to survive in a changing world and produce domestic varieties that would help human societies the world over.

Neither humans nor random mutations can produce new features in dogs or orchids; they merely unveil that which has been hidden in the original design. It seems reasonable to conclude that God placed this genetic variety into animals so that when humans revealed it visibly, they would see reminders of His invisible glory.

BEST FRIENDS! As mentioned before, people have developed nearly 500 breeds of dogs in the last 500 years, each with its own unique suite of traits—both physical and behavioral—to benefit humans. Modern genetic studies show that the breeds draw their traits from four broad categories (wolflike, herders, hunters, and guards). Yet each breed has its own unique mix of DNA.

For a subspecies to acquire this vast genetic variation over such a short time is surprising to evolutionary researchers. They cannot explain so many well-blended traits by slow changes. These suites indicate that dog DNA was designed with great genetic variety and flexiblity that can be observed under different breeding conditions. Clearly the Creator knew mankind would need a "best friend (or friends)."

WOLFLIKE

HERDERS

HUNTERS

NOTE: The amount of coloring in the bars shows how much of a dog's genes align with that trait.

GUARDS

Shiba Inu
Chow Chow
Akita
Alaskan Malamute
Basenji
Shar-pei
Siberian Husky
Afghan Hound
Saluki
Tibetan Terrier
Lhasa Apso
Samoyed
Pekingese
Shih Tzu
Irish Wolfhound
Saint Bernard
Greyhound
Belgian Sheepdog
Belgian Tervuren
Borzoi
Collie
Shetland Sheepdog
Pug
Komondor
Whippet
Standard Poodle
Bichon Frise
Keeshond
Manchester Terrier
Norwegian Elkhound
Kuwasz
Great Dane
Welsh Springer Spaniel
Doberman Pinscher
Standard Schnauzer
Miniature Schnauzer
Australian Terrier
English Cocker Spaniel
Irish Setter
West Highland White Terrier
Pointer
Basset Hound
Cavallier King Charles Spaniel
Giant Schnauzer
Pharaoh Hound
Golden Retriever
Beagle
Bloodhound
Airedale Terrier
American Cocker Spaniel
American Hairless Terrier
Chesapeake Bay Retriever
Cairn Terrier
Portuguese Water Dog
German Shorthand Pointer
Border Collie
Bedlington Terrier
Clumber Spaniel
Ibizan Hound
Rhodesian Ridgeback
Dachshund
Australian Shepherd
Chihuahua
Kerry Blue Terrier
Irish Terrier
Flat Coated Retriever
Soft Coated Wheaten Terrier
Pomeranian
Labrador Retriever
Presa Canario
Rottweiler
Bullmastiff
Newfoundland
German Shepherd
French Bulldog
Miniature Bull Terrier
Bulldog
Boxer
Mastiff
Bernese Mountain Dog
Greater Swiss Mountain Dog

Siberian Husky
Traits of wolf-like dogs include a **high intelligence, strength, and solid companionship.**

Collie
Traits of herding dogs include a great ability to control the movement of other animals and deep loyalty.

Golden Retriever
Traits of hunting dogs include active metabolism, alert nature, and remarkable instincts in the water and woods.

Rottweiler
Traits of guard dogs include strength, intelligence, and fierce loyalty to watch over property.

Heidi G. Parker et al., Science 304:1160; photos: Eric Isselle; cynoclub; GlobalP | Thinkstockphotos.com

33

What can a bear's life tell us about kinds?

[**GRIZZLY BEAR** + **POLAR BEAR** = **GROLAR BEAR**]

On June 29, 2009, *National Geographic* aired a program called "Mystery Bear of the Arctic." The show detailed a most bizarre and unusual find that has been traveling the international news circuit since 2006. It was April 16 of that year, on the south end of Banks Island, that a 65-year-old hunter shot and killed the first documented grizzly/polar hybrid (grolar bear) in the wild. DNA results confirmed that this creature was a product of a male grizzly (*Ursus arctos*) and a female polar bear (*Ursus maritimus*).[1] The anomalous animal was mostly white with brown splotches but had the grizzly traits of long claws, concave face, and humped back.

BEARS OF THE WORLD! The word *bear* finds its origins in the Indo-European root *bher*. From ancient times bears have captivated the imagination. People have cherished their likeness as toys, political emblems, and symbols of strength and great courage. They have also been feared and misunderstood, and this led to their widespread elimination.[2] Because of extensive killing and habitat destruction, the survival of many species is a conservation concern, which is why they are probably the most studied carnivore.[3]

[Polar Bear]

[Giant Panda]

[Spectacled Bear]

[Brown Bear]

[Sloth Bear]

ARK BEARS

[American Black Bear]

[Asian Black Bear]

[Sun Bear]

It is believed in creation biology that Jesus created His creatures to persist.[4] After Noah released the animals, the world they reentered was not the same. It was a devastated world in the throes of a divine judgment, the magnitude of which had never been seen before nor has it been seen since. Ecosystems were different and in constant change for long periods of time. It was a world where God's creatures had to be able to adapt to new and drastically changing conditions.[5,6]

Therefore, it makes sense that these creatures were endowed by their Creator with great genetic diversity and the ability to change with fluctuating environmental conditions. Exciting new research continues to suggest that genetic changes affecting the survival of an organism may not be random, but directed, in the presence of certain environmental cues. This is a direct prediction of a biblical creation model.

THE BEAR NECESSITIES! Bears are known for their adaptability to new environments and food sources. Recent observations made in 2003 and 2004 documented roaming grizzlies regularly visiting the polar bear's traditional domain of the Canadian Arctic Archipelago and riding on sea ice.[7]

SO REMEMBER! Worldview is critical to how we interpret the creation around us. Worldview affects our scientific interpretations, and these interpretations are at the heart of the creation/evolution issue. This issue is not about "science versus religion," but a struggle between a biblical worldview that states that life is designed versus a humanistic worldview that states that life is random. As Christians who enjoy science, we have the Word of the Creator, endorsed by the Lord Jesus Christ, as our foundation upon which we build our creation models. Scientific models come and go, but the Word of the Lord stands forever.

6 What is variation within created kinds?

The true weight of evidence points to "variation within the created kinds." Could there be enough variation in two created human beings, for example, to produce all the variation among human beings we see today? Answer: "Yes, indeed!"

Let's look at human skin color, as an example. First of all, it may surprise you to learn that all of us (except albinos) have exactly the same skin-coloring agent. It's a protein called melanin. How long would it take to get all the variation in skin shade we see among people today? A million years? No. A thousand years? No. Answer: just one generation!

From parents (Adam and Eve) created with medium brown skin shade, all the variation we see today could be produced in one generation. In the same way, plants and animals created with a mixture of genes could have filled all of the earth's ecologic and geographic variety. As people break up into groups, however, some groups would develop limited variability—only dark, only medium, or only light shades of skin.

GOD's Word Says...

God, who made the world and everything in it, since He is Lord of heaven and earth, does not dwell in temples made with hands. Nor is He worshiped with men's hands, as though He needed anything, since He gives to all life, breath, and all things. And He has made from one blood every nation of men to dwell on all the face of the earth, and has determined their preappointed times and the boundaries of their dwellings… (Acts 17:24–26)

CREATED DIVERSITY AND ADAPTATION

According to the creation concept, each kind starts with a large gene pool present. When the descendant populations from these created kinds became isolated, they often became more specialized as they adapted to different environments. Most of this probably occurred after the Flood. Thus, the created ancestors of dogs, for example, have produced such varieties in nature as wolves, coyotes, and jackals. Human beings, of course, have great diversity, too. As the Bible says, God made of "one blood" all the "tribes and tongues and nations" of the earth.

The Bible doesn't tell us what skin shade our first parents had, but, from a design point of view, the medium brown tone can account for the many different tones we see today. Starting with medium-toned parents, it would take only one generation to produce all the variation we see in human skin shades today. In fact, this is the normal situation in India today. Some Indians are as dark as the darkest Africans, and some—perhaps a brother or sister in the same family—as light as the lightest Europeans.

But now notice what happens if human groups were isolated after the Tower of Babel event. If those with very dark skin migrate into the same areas and/or marry only those with very dark skin, then all their children will have very dark skin. Similarly, parents with very light skin can have only very light-skinned children. Where people with different skin shades get together again (as they do in the West Indies, for example), you find the full range of variation again. Clearly, all this is variation within mankind or human kind.

What happened after the Flood and Babel as the descendants of medium-toned parents produced a variety of descendants? Evolution? Not at all. As people multiplied, the genetic variability built right into the first created human beings came to visible expression (along with some variation that has occurred since creation). The darkest Nigerian and the lightest Norwegian, the tallest Watusi and the shortest Pygmy, the highest soprano and the lowest bass could have been present right from the beginning in two people. Great variation in size, color, form, function, etc., would also be present in the created ancestors of all the other kinds (plants and animals) as well.

Varieties within a created kind have the same genes, but different alleles (or versions of the gene). For example, in many Native American tribes, there is a high percentage of blood type A, but that type is quite rare among other tribes. The differences represent different alleles carried by the founders of each tribe as people migrated across the North American continent. All the different varieties of human beings can, of course, marry one another and have children. Many varieties of plants and animals also retain the ability to reproduce, despite differences in appearance as great as those between St. Bernards and Chihuahuas.

7 How could Noah fit the animals on the Ark and care for them?

According to Scripture, Noah's Ark was a safe haven for representatives of all the kinds of air-breathing land animals and birds that God created. While it is possible that God made miraculous provisions for the daily care of these animals, it is not necessary—or required by Scripture—to appeal to miracles. Exploring natural solutions for day-to-day operations does not discount God's role: the biblical account hints at plenty of miracles as written, such as God bringing the animals to the Ark (Genesis 6:20; 7:9, 15), closing the door of the Ark (Genesis 7:16), and causing the fountains of the deep and the windows of heaven to open on the same day (Genesis 7:11). It turns out that a study of existing, low-tech animal care methods answers trivial objections to the Ark. In fact, many solutions to seemingly impossible problems are rather straightforward.

WAS EVERY SPECIES ON THE ARK? To answer this question, we must first ask how many animals were actually on the Ark. Critics have fantasized the presence of millions of animals overloading the Ark. In actuality, the Bible makes it clear that the cargo was limited to land-dwelling, air-breathing animals—corresponding to modern birds, mammals, amphibians, and reptiles, as well as their extinct counterparts. Was every species on the Ark? No! Under these conservative assumptions, there would have been no more than 7,000 land animals and birds on the Ark, and probably less.

According to the Bible, the Ark had three decks (floors). It is not difficult to show that there was plenty of room for several thousand animals, assuming they required approximately the same floor space as animals in typical farm enclosures and laboratories today. The vast majority of the creatures (birds, reptiles, amphibians, and mammals) are small.

It is still necessary to take account of the floor spaces required by large animals, such as elephants, giraffes, rhinos, and some dinosaurs. But even these, collectively, do not require a large area. God would likely have sent to Noah young (and therefore small, but not newborn) representatives of these kinds so that they would have a full reproductive potential for life after the Flood to repopulate the earth (Genesis 7:1–3). Even the largest dinosaurs were relatively small when only a few years old.

This is a cross-section view of a possible design of the interior of the Ark. The proposed skylight roof could be opened. This might be the covering when "Noah removed the covering of the ark" (Genesis 8:13).

SO JUST WHAT DID THE ANIMALS EAT?

The young herbivores could have eaten compressed hay, seeds, grains, and other dried plant material. Regarding potential carnivores on the Ark, we often forget that God created their ancestors as vegetarians (Genesis 1:30). Many of the animals we consider carnivores today could have survived on dried fruit or other preserved plant material. It was recently acknowledged that a significant part of the crocodilian diet is fruit, and the same is true for most bears. In fact, very few living animals are strict carnivores (i.e., obligate carnivores), and the ancestral animals on the Ark could have survived their year-long containment as vegetarians. If necessary, meat preserved through means of drying, pickling, salting, or smoking could have been provided.

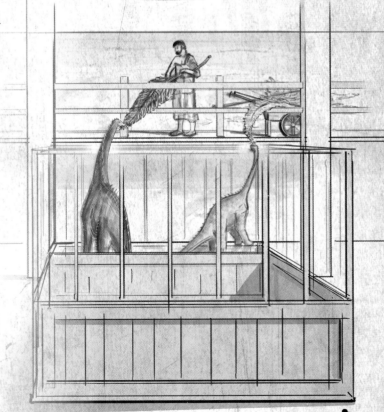

Many critics of the Bible have compared the challenges of caring for the animals with that of modern zoos. This is false. There is a big difference between the long-term care required for animals kept in zoos and the temporary, emergency care required on the Ark. The animals' comfort and healthy appearance were not essential for emergency survival during one stressful year, where survival was the primary goal.

Noah probably stored the food and water near each animal. Even better, drinking water could have been piped into troughs, just as the Chinese have used bamboo pipes for this purpose for thousands of years. The use of some sort of self-feeders, as is commonly done for birds, would have been relatively easy and probably essential. Animals that required special care or diets were uncommon and should not have needed an inordinate amount of time from the handlers. Even animals with the most specialized diets in nature could have been switched to readily sustainable substitute diets. Of course, this assumes that animals with specialized diets today were likewise specialized at the time of the Flood. But that may not have been the case for the ancestral representatives of the kinds taken on the Ark.

RHINOCEROSES The earliest known rhinos were relatively small and hornless or bore small nasal bumps like this *Trigonias*. However, most members of this kind possess at least one facial horn along the midlines of their bodies. Rhino behavior and anatomy is consistent with the biblical descriptions of "unicorns"[2] (Job 39:9–12; Psalm 29:6, KJV).

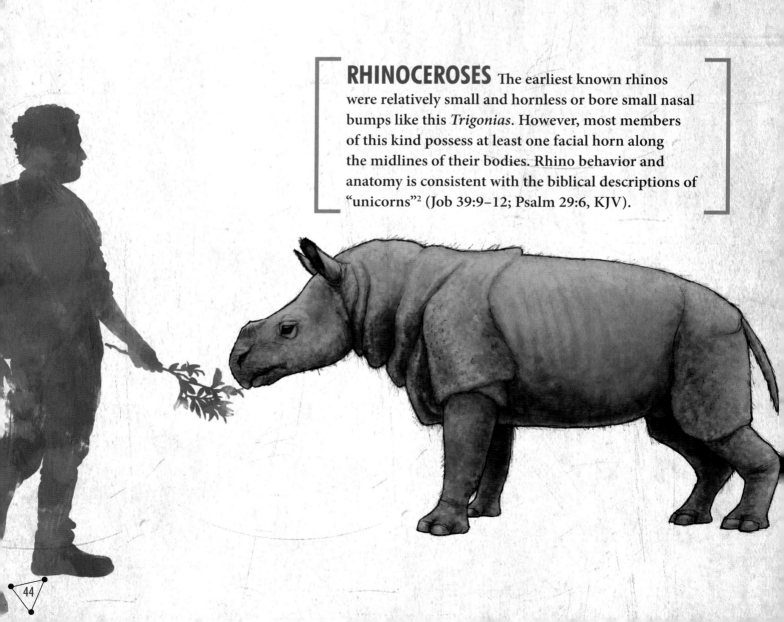

THAT'S A WHOLE LOTTA POO! As much as 6 U.S. tons of animal waste may have been produced daily on the Ark! The key to keeping the enclosures clean was to avoid the need for Noah and his family to do the work. The right systems could also prevent the need to change animal bedding. Noah could have accomplished this in several ways. One possibility would be to allow the waste to accumulate below the animals, much as we see in rustic henhouses. Small animals, such as birds, could have multiple levels in their enclosures, and waste could have simply accumulated at the bottom of each. The danger of toxic or explosive manure gases, such as methane, would be alleviated by the constant movement of the Ark, which would have allowed manure gases to be constantly released. Flat, lip-rimmed floors in animal enclosures would have allowed the waste, given the Ark's movements, to flow into large central gutters and then into collection pits, allowing gravity to do most of the work. Noah's family could have then dumped this overboard without an excessive expenditure of manpower.

Another possibility on the Ark is that the animals may have hibernated during a portion of the voyage. If animals hibernated, this would, of course, have greatly alleviated the need to feed, water, and remove the waste of the Ark animals.

Hibernation was not necessary for the animals to have been adequately cared for on the Ark. It only would have made it easier.

8 Conclusion: How many kinds were there really?

As part of the evangelistic Ark Encounter project, Answers in Genesis has engaged scholars to research how many actual animal kinds would have been needed on Noah's Ark. It is important to understand that the word *kind* used in Genesis 1 seems to represent something closer to the "family" level of classification in most instances, as this book has addressed so clearly.

The following is from Dr. Jean Lightner on this topic, covering living mammal kinds, and published in Answers in Genesis' peer-reviewed *Answers Research Journal*:

> Based on the methods outlined in "Determining the Ark Kinds" (Lightner et al., 2011), information on the class Mammalia was evaluated in an attempt to get a realistic estimate of what mammalian kinds would have been represented on the Ark. Examining information on extant species (those alive today), it was estimated that they represent 137 created kinds. Given the number of extinct mammalian families known from the fossil record, the actual number on the Ark could easily have been well over 300. This estimate is very low compared with those in the past. In evaluating the information, a number of important creationist research questions have been discussed. As further research is undertaken to address these, our knowledge of created kinds will be significantly advanced.

Analysts conducting research for the Ark Encounter project predict that less than 1,400 animal kinds were preserved on Noah's Ark. Since there were only two of most kinds (seven pairs of some—"clean" animals and those capable of powered flight), this means there were likely fewer than 6,700 individual animals on the Ark. This number is much smaller than what people have been claiming over the years.

At the Ark Encounter in Kentucky, people enter the Ark and learn of Noah's intelligence and his ability to build something like this. Then they see all the exhibits, including teaching bays, bays dealing with Noah's family, Noah's life, the pre-Flood world, teaching on how they could feed the animals, and exhibits in regard to waste products from the animals as well.

Other than the Cross, the Ark is the greatest reminder of salvation, for in the judgement God provided salvation to Noah and his family, and in the judgement of sin and death, God provides salvation through Christ's death on the Cross and His resurrection. Jesus said, "I am the door, by me if any man enters in he will be saved" (John 10:9). Just as Noah and his family went through the door to be saved, so we need to go through a door to be saved, and that door is the Lord Jesus Christ.

LET'S DO THE MATH!

There were likely under 1,400 kinds of animals for a total of fewer than 6,700 animals. Here is the breakdown:

NON-FOSSIL	KINDS	PER KIND	TOTAL
AMPHIBIANS	194	2	388
REPTILES	101	2	202
BIRDS	195	flightless 5@2, flight 190@14	2670
MAMMAL	137	unclean 106@2, clean and flying 31@14	646

FOSSIL	KINDS	PER KIND	TOTAL
AMPHIBIANS	54	2	108
REPTILES	211 (projected)	flightless 187@2, flight 24@14	710
BIRDS	89 (projected)	flightless 21@2, flight 68@14	994
SYNAPSIDS	78 (projected)	2	156
MAMMAL	314 (projected)	unclean 301@2, clean and flying 13@14	784
TOTAL	**1,373**		**6,658**

[Megacerops]   [Thylacosmilus]   [Anisodon]   [Cotylorhynchus]   [Quetzalcoatlus]

9 The animal kinds zoo!

As you know, there were probably under 1,400 animal kinds on the Ark! Here are some members of just a few of those kinds.

CYNOGNATHIDS

Historically called "mammal-like reptiles," cynognathids—like this *Cynognathus*—were actually more like mammals than crocodiles or lizards. They are now considered a kind of "non-mammalian synapsid."

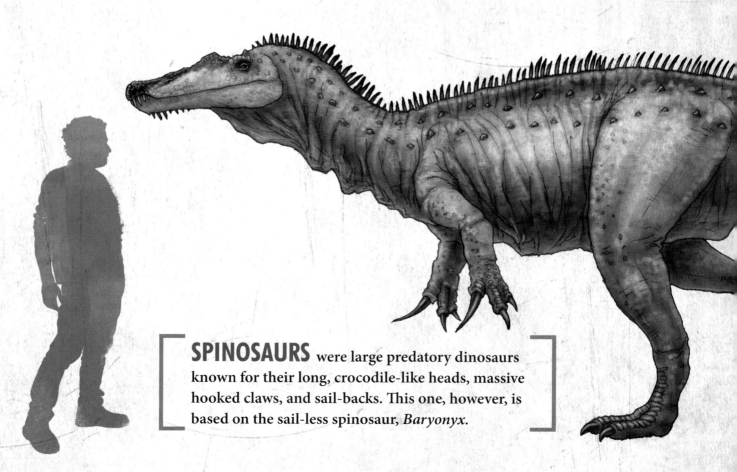

SPINOSAURS were large predatory dinosaurs known for their long, crocodile-like heads, massive hooked claws, and sail-backs. This one, however, is based on the sail-less spinosaur, *Baryonyx*.

ENTELODONTS

Once considered the relatives of pigs, entelodonts were a unique and bizarre animal kind. Known only from pre-Ice Age rock layers, they ranged from two feet tall—such as this *Archaeotherium*—to nearly seven feet tall!

DOGS

Long considered "man's best friend," not every member of the canid family is like our beloved pets. Various wolves, coyotes, jackals, foxes, and wild dogs are also members of the dog kind. There were numerous extinct forms as well, like borophagines—the bone-crushing dogs—and small civet-like canids, like this *Hesperocyon*.

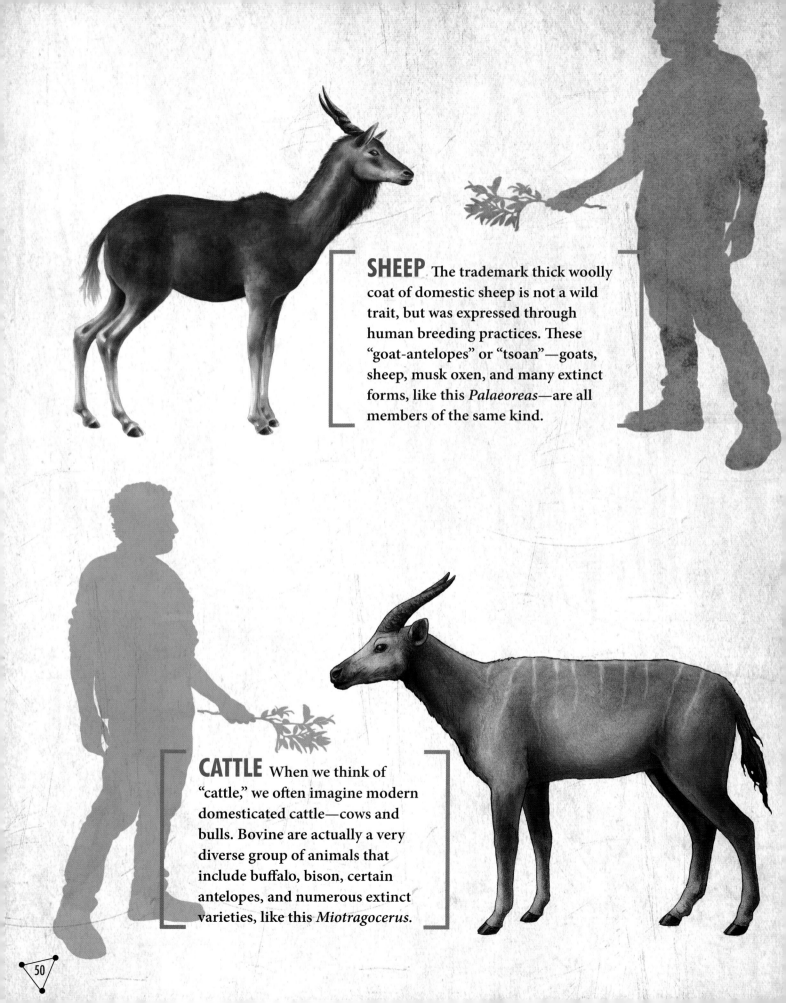

SHEEP The trademark thick woolly coat of domestic sheep is not a wild trait, but was expressed through human breeding practices. These "goat-antelopes" or "tsoan"—goats, sheep, musk oxen, and many extinct forms, like this *Palaeoreas*—are all members of the same kind.

CATTLE When we think of "cattle," we often imagine modern domesticated cattle—cows and bulls. Bovine are actually a very diverse group of animals that include buffalo, bison, certain antelopes, and numerous extinct varieties, like this *Miotragocerus*.

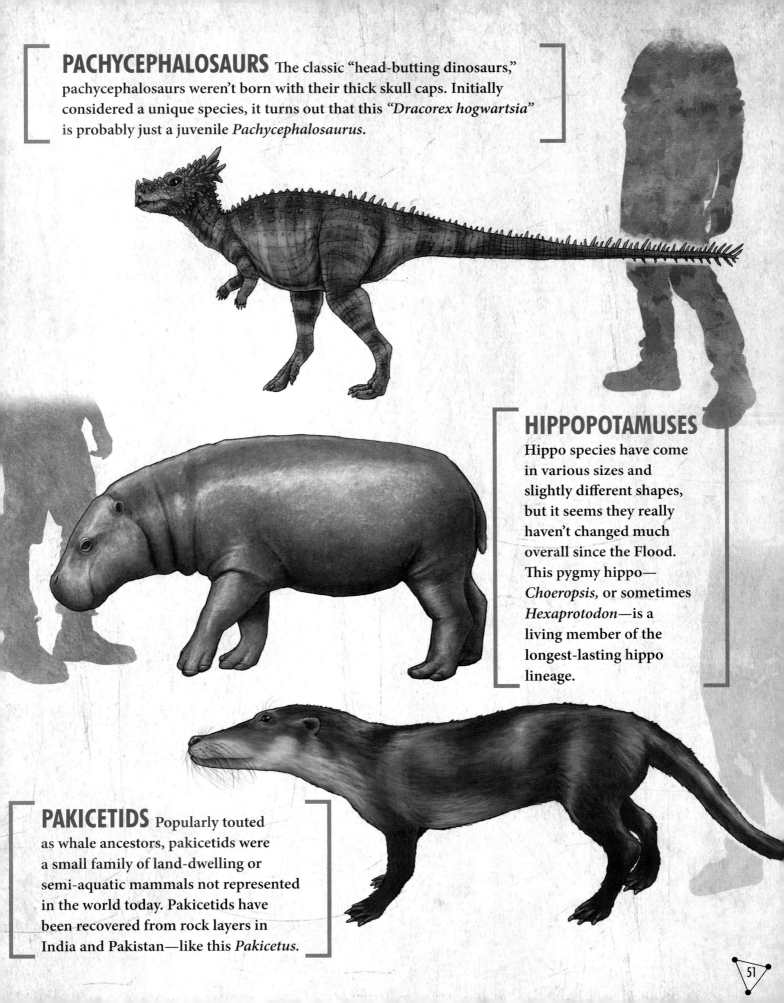

PACHYCEPHALOSAURS

The classic "head-butting dinosaurs," pachycephalosaurs weren't born with their thick skull caps. Initially considered a unique species, it turns out that this *"Dracorex hogwartsia"* is probably just a juvenile *Pachycephalosaurus*.

HIPPOPOTAMUSES

Hippo species have come in various sizes and slightly different shapes, but it seems they really haven't changed much overall since the Flood. This pygmy hippo—*Choeropsis,* or sometimes *Hexaprotodon*—is a living member of the longest-lasting hippo lineage.

PAKICETIDS

Popularly touted as whale ancestors, pakicetids were a small family of land-dwelling or semi-aquatic mammals not represented in the world today. Pakicetids have been recovered from rock layers in India and Pakistan—like this *Pakicetus.*

STAHLECKERIIDS

Many extinct animals looked like the stuff of science fiction. *Placerias*, the stahleckeriid synapsid shown here, was no exception. Its stocky body, short tail, beak, and tusk-like facial flanges made it look quite unlike anything we've seen before.

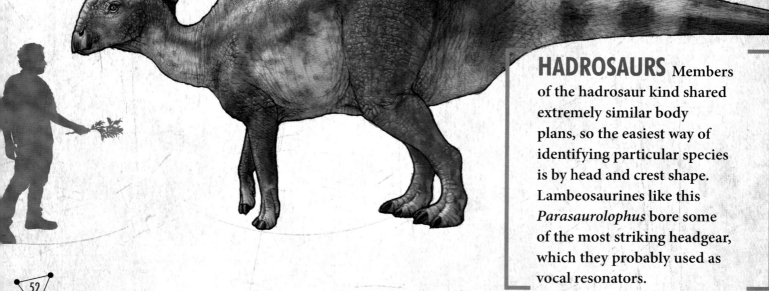

REBBACHISAURS

As far as we know, certain sauropod dinosaurs were the largest animals that ever walked the earth. This one is a rebbachisaurid called *Nigersaurus*—a low-level grazer, like the behemoth described in Job 40:15–24.

HADROSAURS

Members of the hadrosaur kind shared extremely similar body plans, so the easiest way of identifying particular species is by head and crest shape. Lambeosaurines like this *Parasaurolophus* bore some of the most striking headgear, which they probably used as vocal resonators.

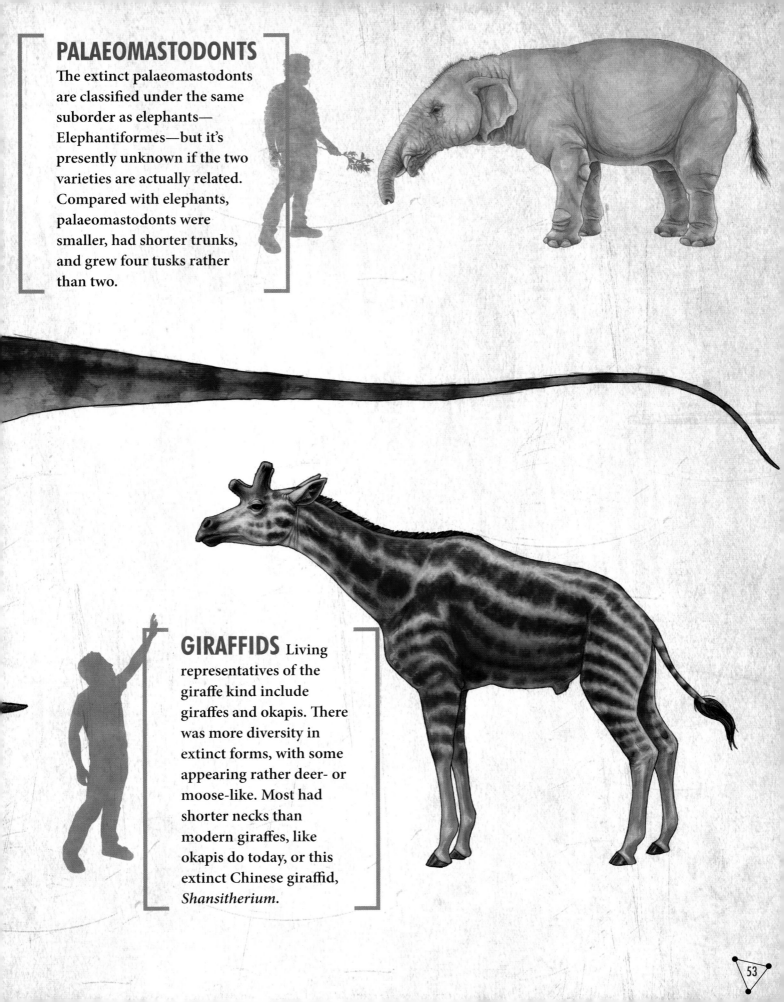

PALAEOMASTODONTS

The extinct palaeomastodonts are classified under the same suborder as elephants—Elephantiformes—but it's presently unknown if the two varieties are actually related. Compared with elephants, palaeomastodonts were smaller, had shorter trunks, and grew four tusks rather than two.

GIRAFFIDS Living representatives of the giraffe kind include giraffes and okapis. There was more diversity in extinct forms, with some appearing rather deer- or moose-like. Most had shorter necks than modern giraffes, like okapis do today, or this extinct Chinese giraffid, *Shansitherium*.

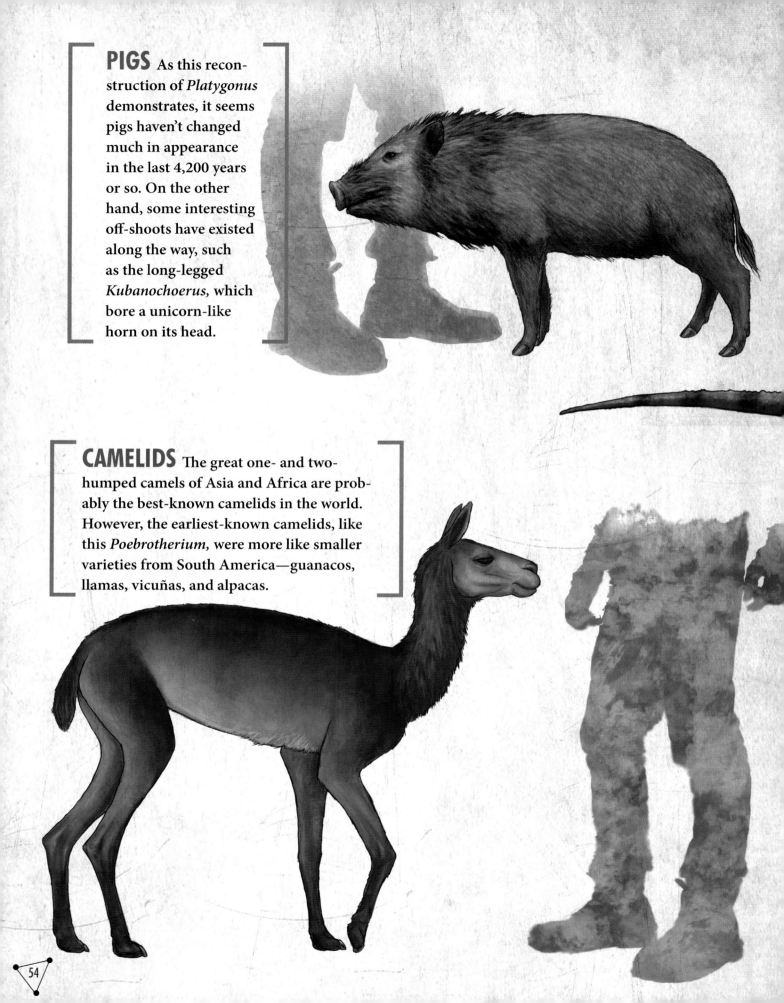

PIGS As this reconstruction of *Platygonus* demonstrates, it seems pigs haven't changed much in appearance in the last 4,200 years or so. On the other hand, some interesting off-shoots have existed along the way, such as the long-legged *Kubanochoerus,* which bore a unicorn-like horn on its head.

CAMELIDS The great one- and two-humped camels of Asia and Africa are probably the best-known camelids in the world. However, the earliest-known camelids, like this *Poebrotherium,* were more like smaller varieties from South America—guanacos, llamas, vicuñas, and alpacas.

CATS Today, the cat kind is represented by felines, like cheetahs, and pantherines, like lions. In the past, there was greater variation, with machairodontines—such as the saber-toothed cat—and proailurines, like this *Proailurus*.

SILESAURS It's good to remember that not every extinct animal that looked like a dinosaur actually was a dinosaur. Such was the case with silesaurs, like this *Silesaurus*. Although it was a "dinosauriform," certain aspects of its neck, arms, and hips exclude it from the superorder Dinosauria.

SIMOSUCHUS was a pug-nosed, short-tailed, crocodile-like reptile. At maturity, they were less than three feet in length and covered with bony plates, called scutes. They were apparently plant-eaters, exhibiting leaf-shaped buckteeth set in boxy skulls—not what you think of when you hear "crocodile."

STEGOSAURS One of the most popular dinosaur groups in the world are the stegosaurs. This kind included at least two subfamilies and numerous species, but the classic form is still the original: *Stegosaurus,* shown here. Fossil evidence confirms that their spikes were used as weapons, while their plates were likely display and body heat-regulating organs.

UINTATHERES At first glance, uintatheres probably looked a lot like rhinos. These two groups are completely unrelated, however, and the differences become obvious with closer examination. For instance, many uintatheres had tusks, ossicones like giraffes, and elephant-like feet.

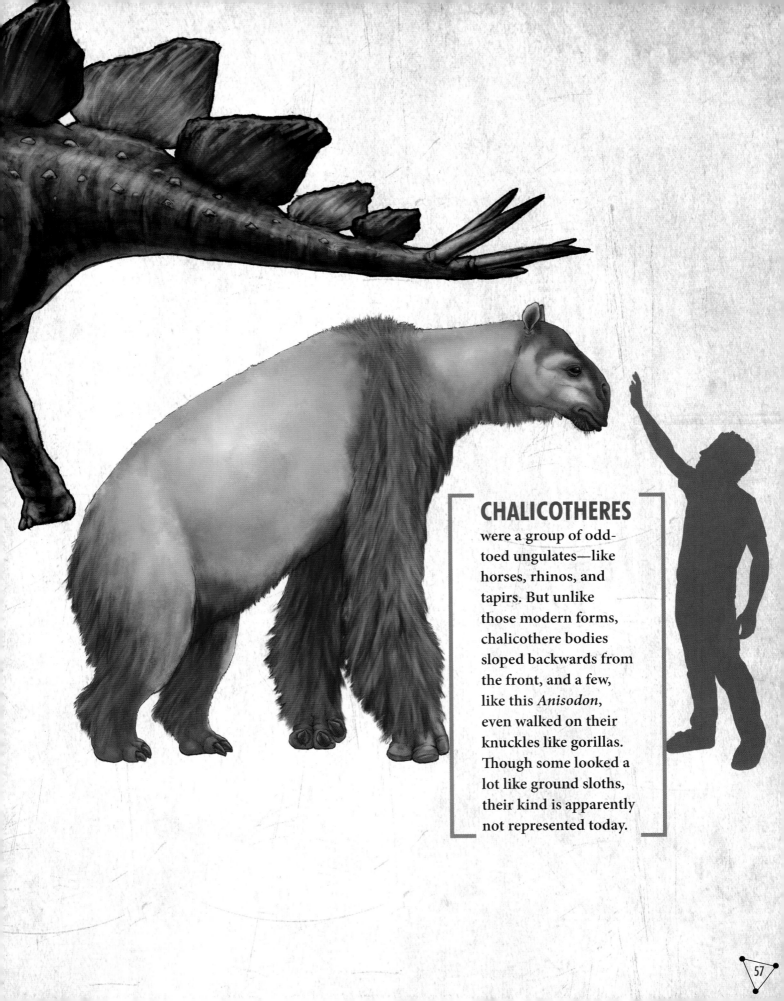

CHALICOTHERES

were a group of odd-toed ungulates—like horses, rhinos, and tapirs. But unlike those modern forms, chalicothere bodies sloped backwards from the front, and a few, like this *Anisodon*, even walked on their knuckles like gorillas. Though some looked a lot like ground sloths, their kind is apparently not represented today.

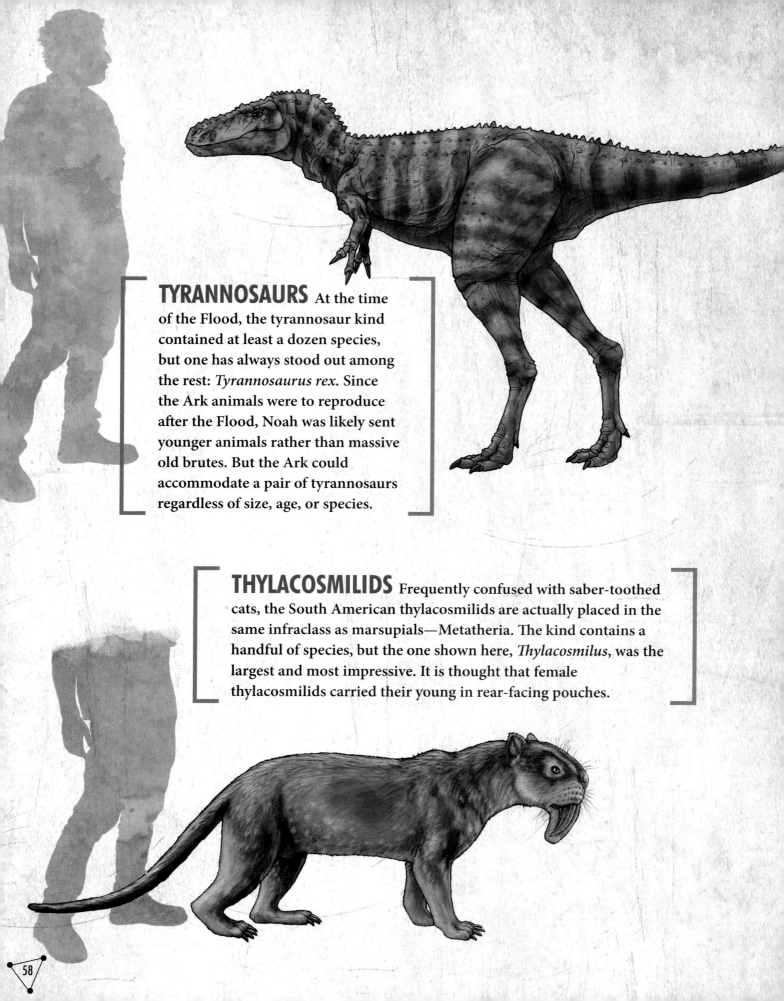

TYRANNOSAURS At the time of the Flood, the tyrannosaur kind contained at least a dozen species, but one has always stood out among the rest: *Tyrannosaurus rex*. Since the Ark animals were to reproduce after the Flood, Noah was likely sent younger animals rather than massive old brutes. But the Ark could accommodate a pair of tyrannosaurs regardless of size, age, or species.

THYLACOSMILIDS Frequently confused with saber-toothed cats, the South American thylacosmilids are actually placed in the same infraclass as marsupials—Metatheria. The kind contains a handful of species, but the one shown here, *Thylacosmilus*, was the largest and most impressive. It is thought that female thylacosmilids carried their young in rear-facing pouches.

Endnotes

Except for chapter 2, these chapters are adapted from articles on the Answers in Genesis website: www.answersingenesis.org

Chapter 1

https://answersingenesis.org/creation-science/baraminology/variety-within-created-kinds/

Chapter 2

Adapted from: Parker, Gary. *Building Blocks in Life Science.* Green Forest, AR: Master Books, 2011.

Chapter 3

https://answersingenesis.org/hybrid-animals/zonkeys-ligers-and-wolphins-oh-my/

1. Some might argue that if the hybrid offspring are infertile, then this indicates that the parent animals are of separate created kinds. However, fertility of the offspring has no bearing on the kind designation. Hybridization is the key.
2. Stephen Adams, "Dolphin and Whale Mate to Create a 'Wholphin,'" Telegraph.co.uk website news, April 2, 2008, Telegraph Media Group Limited, www.telegraph.co.uk/news/uknews/1582973/Dolphin-and-whale-mate-to-create-a-wolphin.html.

Chapter 4

https://answersingenesis.org/creation-science/baraminology/suite-dogs/

1. http://www.americanscientist.org/issues/id.3724,y.2007,no.5,content.true,page.1,css.print/issue.aspx
2. http://www.asa3.org/ASA/PSCF/2001/PSCF9-01Miles.html
3. Adam Freedman et al., "Genome Sequencing Highlights the Dynamic Early History of Dogs," PLoS Genetics; 10 (1): e1004016 DOI: 10.1371/journal.pgen.
4. The appendix in Jean Lighter's "Mammalian Ark Kinds," *Answers Research Journal 5* (2012): 151–204, lists 13 living genera and 35 living species in Canidae. When extinct species were included, the total rose to 57 genera and 153 species.
5. Kurt P. Wise, *Devotional Biology: Learning to Worship the Creator of Organisms* (Truett-McConnell College Press: 2013); biology textbook used for Truett-McConnell College students.
6. Some evolutionists disdain the Russian research because it does not emphasize the full impact humans can have on dog evolution. Humans prefer "random" traits, such as spotted (piebald) fur, that are not good for wild animals needing camouflage. Once humans select animals with these traits, they must continually protect them from wild predators.
7. http://ngm.nationalgeographic.com/2011/03/taming-wild-animals/ratliff-text/2

Chapter 5

https://answersingenesis.org/hybrid-animals/interpreting-unusual-arctic-bear-in-creation-model-of-origins/

1. Photo in the News: Polar Bear-Grizzly Hybrid Discovered, accessed 30 June 2009.
2. Vaughn, M.V. and Fuller, T.K. ed., Ursus Volume 11, A selection of papers from the 11th International Conference on Bear Research and Management (Graz, Austria: International Association for Bear Research and Management, 1999), p. 22.
3. Krause, J., Unger, T., Nocon, A., Sapfo-Malaspinas, A., Orestis-Kolokotronos, S., Stiller, M., Soibelzon, L., Spriggs, H., Dear, P.H., Briggs, A.W., Bray, S.C.E., O'Brien, S.J., Rabeder, G., Matheus, P., Cooper, A., Slatkin, M., Pääbo, S., and Hofreiter, M., Mitochondrial Genomes Reveal an Explosive Radiation of Extinct and Extant Bears near the Miocene-Pliocene Boundary, BMC Evolutionary Biology 8 no. 220 (2008), Pub. Online doi:10.1186/1471-2148-8-220.
4. Genesis 1, Isaiah 45:18
5. Hennigan, T., Purdom, G. and Wood, T.C., Creation's Hidden Potential, Answers, January–March 2009, pp. 70–75.
6. Lightner, J., Life: Designed by God to Adapt, Answers in Depth 3 (2008).
7. Doupé, J.P., England, J.H., Furze, M., Paetkau, D., Most Northerly Observation of a Grizzly Bear (Ursus arctos) in Canada: Photographic and DNA Evidence from Melville Island, Northwest Territories, Arctic 60 no. 3 (2007): 271–276.

Chapter 6

https://answersingenesis.org/creation-science/baraminology/variation-yes-evolution-no/

Chapter 7

https://answersingenesis.org/noahs-ark/caring-for-the-animals-on-the-ark/
1. https://answersingenesis.org/extinct-animals/unicorns-in-the-bible/

Chapter 8

https://answersingenesis.org/blogs/ken-ham/2012/11/01/how-many-kinds/

Image Credit

T-top, B-bottom, L-left, R-right, C-Center

Shutterstock.com: p. 2, p. 3, p. 4, p. 6, p. 7, p. 9, p. 11, p. 12, p. 13T, B, p 14, p. 15, p. 16, p. 17, p. 18, p. 19T, p. 20T, p. 21, p. 22, p. 23, p. 24, p. 25, p 26, p. 28, p. 29 p. 30, p. 31, p. 32, p. 33, p. 34B, p. 35, p. 36, p. 37,

istock.com:, p. 13 BL, p. 35 (kermode bear), p. 38T, P. 39, p. 40, p. 41,

Dreamstime.com: p. 26CR

Answers in Genesis: p. 42, p. 43, p. 45,

John Einselen: p. 5T,
Joel Briggs: p. 29 C (Ark dog), p. 36C (Ark bears), p. 44, p.48-58
Tim Hansen: p. 47

Bill Looney: p. 19B

National Geographic Creative: Zigmund Leszczynski / Animals Animals/Earth Scenes/National Geographic Creative p. 21 Tigon

Science Photo Library: Natural History Museum, London / Science Source p. 34T

Wikimedia Commons: Images from Wikimedia Commons are used under the CC-BY-SA-3.0 license (or previous creative commons licenses) or the GNU Free Documentation License, Version 1.3. U.S.

p. 8T, p. 10T, p. 12 (red wolf), p. 20B, p. 27, p. 31 (Arabian wolf)

The Ark Encounter is a one-of-a-kind, historically-themed attraction that features a full size, all wood Ark.

Located in Williamstown, Kentucky, the Ark Encounter is the largest timber-frame structure in the USA, with three levels and over 130 exhibit bays within the ship. The experience points to the feasibility of Noah's Ark and the authority of God's Word.

ARK ENCOUNTER®

NOAH'S ARK
THINKING OUTSIDE THE BOX

by TIM LOVETT

$15.99 U.S.
C 978-0-89051-507-5

FIGURING OUT THE DESIGN

Genesis might be an abbreviated version of God's instructions about the ark, or perhaps Noah was smart enough to fill in the details himself. In either case, we are encouraged to investigate (Prov. 25:2 "It is the glory of God to conceal a matter; to search out a matter is the glory of kings."). There are three places to look — the Bible, testable science, and tradition.

The Bible: The reliable, yet sometimes brief, record of Noah's ark.

Testable Science: Engineering principles might help to fill in more detail and hopefully bring us closer to God's complete specifications (or Noah's ingenuity). Designing a ship requires a balance of many factors. Some are essential (like staying afloat), while others are only preferable (like ease of construction).

Essential factors: Won't leak, break, or capsize. Ride is not dangerously rough. Can be built with available technology. Houses all the animals and food safely.

Preferable factors: Optimized for a comfortable ride and best living conditions. Ease of construction. Low maintenance during voyage.

Another form of testable science is an artifact, but nothing has been found of Noah's ark. However, we do have artifacts from ancient ships that match historical records. These might hold clues since Noah's ark was the first ship in our (post-flood) history.

Tradition: Clues might be gleaned from Flood legends and ancient technologies.

True operational science should not conflict with the Bible. Unfortunately, even operational science can make mistakes, in which case the Bible overrules. Likewise, it would be wise to let operational science overrule legends.

Clearly the challenges Noah faced were daunting. Little is known of Noah or of the engineering abilities, tools, or craftsmanship of people of the time.

Make yourself an ark of gopherwood; make rooms in the ark, and cover it inside and outside with pitch. And this is how you shall make it: The length of the ark shall be three hundred cubits, its width fifty cubits, and its height thirty cubits. You shall make a window for the ark, and you shall finish it to a cubit from above; and set the door of the ark in its side. You shall make it with lower, second, and third decks. (Gen. 6:14–16).

Faithful to the biblical dimensions, Lovett reveals a feasible ark design, explores the impact of Flood waters on the vessel, and provides remarkable insight into the skills and techniques needed to construct it.

Master Books®
A Division of New Leaf Publishing Group
www.masterbooks.com

Here one can see the progress being made as the Amish team puts together more bents. The first one took two weeks to assemble and raise into place. They were eventually able to do two in a week's time.

The Ark construction with six bents fully in place.

Now with 15 bents in place, and starting on the outer skin as well.

THE BUILDING OF THE
ARK ENCOUNTER
BY FAITH HE BUILT THE ARK

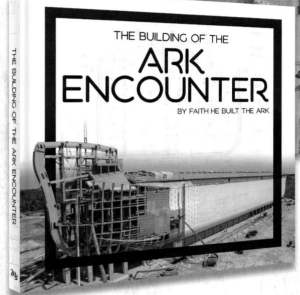

Discover details of this engineering masterpiece as the largest timberframed building in the world. At 510 feet long, 85 feet wide, and 51 feet high based on the Bible's dimensions, it presents the world with an awe-inspiring reminder of the scriptural account of the Ark.

$17.99 U.S.
C 978-0-89051-931-8

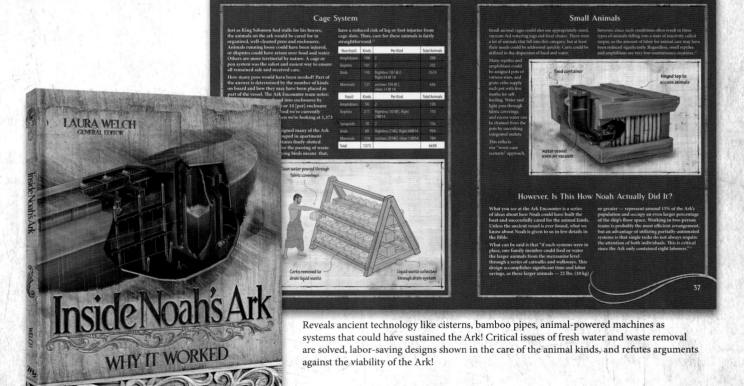

LAURA WELCH
GENERAL EDITOR

Inside Noah's Ark
WHY IT WORKED

Reveals ancient technology like cisterns, bamboo pipes, animal-powered machines as systems that could have sustained the Ark! Critical issues of fresh water and waste removal are solved, labor-saving designs shown in the care of the animal kinds, and refutes arguments against the viability of the Ark!

$16.99 U.S.
C 978-0-89051-932-5

THE VOYAGE BEGINS AGAIN

Williamstown, KY, South of Cincinnati

ArkEncounter.com